A PUB

Despising the Shame

Living Beyond the Damage of Childhood Sexual Abuse: One Survivor's Story

By
Sallie Culbreth, M.S.
Founder
Committed to Freedom

Committed to Freedom provides spiritual tools to help people move beyond abuse, exploitation, and sexual trauma. For more information:
Committed to Freedom
PO Box 20916
Hot Springs, AR 71903 USA
www.committedtofreedom.org
© 2013

To
Tim, Anne, Dan, and my Family

*Thanks for permitting me
to be the poster child*

With gratitude to
**Cathy, Paula, Kristy, Scott, Cindy,
Doris, Sam, Patty, Dave, Jerry, and Nan**

***I will repay you for the years
the locusts have eaten***
*Joel 2:25
Hebrew Bible (NIV)*

Introduction

Collage of images from the house where I was abused in Arkadelphia, Arkansas

Unfortunately, my story is not very unusual. Sadly, it is a very common tale. I offer no explicit, sensational descriptions that distinguish my experiences of sexual abuse as more horrific or less traumatizing than another person's story.

I am a survivor – perhaps like you. That is my reality. But I have come to understand this much: *I am more than the abuse.* I have scars from it. It shaped me. I was forced to fight unfair battles, but I am more. I despise what I had to work through to come to that conclusion, but the roads I travelled led me to a place of empowerment and freedom.

And so I tell my common story to give you a small glimpse into a very complicated journey. This is not a tell-all book and the journey will continue for me. That's because I haven't finished growing. Like you, I am a work in progress.

Along my journey I found understanding and support. I also found spiritual healing as I reconsidered the experiences of Jesus who, like me, carried shame that was not his own. I found an advocate whose journey into darkness opened my eyes to light. As you read this, for whatever reason, I pray that you will be able to look beyond what was done to me, and focus deeply on *now*. It is this *now* that is the glory of this very common tale.

Peace,

Sallie

Smaller Than the Memories

I found myself in Arkadelphia, Arkansas with some unexpected time on my hands one Saturday. My daughter needed a ride to Henderson State University where the A.C.T. test was being administered. Our forty-five minute drive from Hot Springs was uneventful and fairly quiet as we both tried to wake up for an early weekend morning. Once I dropped her off, I realized there were three hours for me to kill and I had nothing to do. No book to read. No project to plan. No meeting to attend. It was odd for me to be in such a situation, but I was. Three hours of test-taking torment for my daughter. Three hours of free time for me.

Arkadelphia is a very small, southern town – a college town that has not one, but two universities. Other than the schools, there really isn't too much to it. I drove around aimlessly for awhile, but kept feeling a nudge to do something I had never planned to do – find the house where my grandfather sexually abused me as a child. I wondered if I could find it.

Decades had passed since then, yet the damage that remained from his actions had survived through all those years. In fact the damage had not only survived, but had grown, taking on a life of its own. I had been forever altered by his actions and had carried his shame for so long, that it finally became my own.

Like a machine that pulls salt water taffy, my thoughts and memories were churning as I drove. Up one street, down another. Nothing looked familiar, and yet, everything was very familiar. From the corner of my eye, I caught a glimpse of Rose Hill cemetery. I slowed, trying hard to remember why it was important, why I felt as if I knew it. On a whim, I turned the corner and shuttled back and forth along the streets near the cemetery. I wound around curves, taking corners, changing directions. Slowing down. Speeding up. I began to recognize small things, pieces of my childhood that were coming together in my mind and making more sense to me. I knew I was very close. I passed the church we had belonged to – Second Baptist Church on South 12th Street. I remembered it. I remembered going to Sunday School and Bible Quiz.

Block after block, the anticipation grew. Why was I doing this? I had made so much progress in my journey away from this place and the awful things that happened to me here, why did I want to open all that back up? Closure? Confrontation? That would have been impossible because both of my grandparents were dead by then. The only confrontation would have taken place between me and the shadows that were formed a lifetime ago. I don't know, I guess I just needed to see it. To know if I was strong enough, free enough to come and then go. To be empowered by the fact that I could drive away when I chose to do so.

Another turn and I was back on the South 12th Street, but several blocks down from the cemetery and the church. It was a dead end road and I remembered it! I slowed to a crawl, studying every house. Was that it? Was it this one? That one? And then, I stopped. The engine idled, awaiting my instructions, but I gave none. My foot was heavy on the brake as I leaned down to look through my windshield. That was it all right. My grandparents' house.

I pulled over to the opposite side of the street and parked across from the house. After several minutes, I turned off the car. The silence and air pressure in the car deafened me. I waited for some sort of monumental emotion to take hold of me. Rage. Sadness. Relief. Closure. I felt none of those things. I felt nothing. Not the kind of nothing that comes because of denial or dissociation. I simply had no feelings about what I was seeing.

For many years, I had been working hard to move beyond my abuse, and suddenly, I was there. Staring at it. Studying the house. Was it occupied? By whom? Did they know what happened there? Did the neighbors know? Those were my only thoughts. Just thoughts, but no real feelings.

I scanned the other small houses close by, and one just across the street looked occupied. In fact, I noticed someone peering from behind the front window curtains, but quickly disappeared when we caught a glimpse of each other. I got out of the car and knocked on the door. An elderly woman in a house duster, pink foam hair curlers, and house shoes opened the door a few inches.

I introduced myself and told her my grandparents used to live in that house. I asked if she knew them. She did. I asked if she knew the current occupants. She didn't know them well and wasn't quite sure of their names. I thanked her and just as I turned to leave she said, "You know, it's the strangest thing. Ever since your grandparents moved out of that house, no one has ever been able to stay in it for very long. I don't know why. People move in, then move out pretty quickly."

I walked across the street and stood in front of it. It was just a house. A small, insignificant house at the end of a dead-end street. Nothing spectacular. Not the house in *The Haunting* or *Psycho* or *Nightmare on Elm Street.* It was an old, simple, modest small southern house with magnolia trees, poison ivy, and kudzu vines on the outer edges of the yard. And then it dawned on me.

The house was much smaller than my memories.

If Walls Could Talk

    The organization I founded, Committed to Freedom, was growing. New challenges lay before me with this growth. Funding. Promotion. Writing. Schedules. Staff. How could I communicate the uncomfortable realities of sexual assault without being graphic? It occurred to me that the perfect backdrop for a promotional video was in front of the Arkadelphia house. After all, I'd already seen it. Already confronted my past, driven away, and left it behind me. I discussed the idea with my family and several friends who had been on this journey with me for quite some time. None of us had any doubt. To stand in front of the house where I was abused and share the vision of Committed to Freedom would be an extremely powerful visual image.

    The first step was to obtain permission from the house owner to film there. I drove the familiar roads from Hot Springs to Arkadelphia, retracing the path I had taken three years earlier. Not knowing who lived there, I decided to invite a colleague to accompany me. We had some work to discuss that could be accomplished on the forty-five minute drive, so I thought we could kill two birds with one stone. Efficient use of our time, right?

The plan was to knock on the door with a written request to film in the front yard. Once I obtained their consent, we would drive back to Hot Springs. That was the plan. Quick. Simple. Uneventful. I had no way of knowing what awaited me there.

The cemetery snaked by as we turned the corner. The grave markers felt unexpectedly ominous, like stone sentinels of loss that had taken place on that dead-end road. Loss of innocence. Loss of childhood. Loss of trust. Loss of faith. The car slowed. My heart quickened. Gravel and asphalt crunched under the tires. I lowered the window to breathe in the small town air and perhaps hear the whispered testimonies of those entombed souls or my buried memories. Rather than faint echoes, the noise from times long past grew too loud for me and I quickly rolled up the window.

In slow motion, I turned away from the granite monuments and toward the road that carried us to the house. I felt strange. Like an awaiting open grave, I was filled with dread. I could almost hear something calling me to climb back in and die all over again.

We drove through the haphazardly placed little houses that had sprouted in a neighborhood with no apparent forethought. Despite my inexplicable apprehension, nothing seemed unusual. It was the picture of Mayberry Americana. Then the road ran out and the car rolled to a stop.

I could barely comprehend what I saw.

There, where the road ran into an end, was the house. My grandparents' house. The one I had faced a few years before with very little emotion. The one that was much smaller than my memories. But it had changed. It had been blown apart, ripped open, and shattered. The only house in the slapdash neighborhood hit by the powerful tornado of 1997 was this one. The *only* one! Yes, other houses throughout the area had been demolished by that same tornado, but that fact blurred into the background. The one house I came for had been obliterated.

The destruction felt familiar. Its isolation, I knew all too well. By then, the structure had been abandoned for several years, left to decay, alone and unnoticed. I understood. I, too, felt like the only one who had ever been touched by such destruction, left to decay from a storm I never invited.

I was completely unprepared for the impact this would have on me. That eerie sensation I felt as we passed the cemetery settled deep in my soul. Looking at the shattered, decomposing house felt like I was staring back into that open grave I had sensed a few blocks back. The occupants had vacated long ago, replaced by vines and rot, water, vandals, and stray animals. I opened the car door. A gust of wind blasted against me and the real world drifted away. I was no longer a middle aged woman. I was a little girl. No car. No colleague. No people. No protection. Just me. Alone and small.

At first, I circled the house through knee high brown grass. I had not ventured so close to it a few years earlier. As if trying to touch a wounded, wild animal, I approached with great caution. Even if the creature had been disabled, the danger still felt very real. My flesh bristled. Every nerve was on high alert. I felt *his* presence – not God's presence – *his* – my grandfather.

Images from the past superimposed themselves over the present. There I was, a child playing in the yard with my cousins and little brother. Happy children, carefree and giddy. Then, I was plunged into a very dark place, but flashbacks like strobe lights brought other scenes into my view, crowding out the playing children. Grandpa cruelly torturing a cocker spaniel. Grandpa tormenting and terrifying my little brother. My mother, trying to defend my brother. My mousy grandmother who did nothing to protect any of us. Loud arguments and horrible words flying from his mouth to Mother, to me and my brother. Fleeing to the car to escape. Trembling. Sobbing. Getting away as fast as we could.

I squeezed my eyes closed as hard as I could, trying to expunge the images that came while standing at the back of that house. My pace quickened to get back around to the front, as if I could outrun the phantom yard scenes. I could hardly breathe. I gasped for air and steadied myself. Back around front, where that magnolia tree once stood, was now just a trunk, snapped in half. A kitchen knife had impaled it, buried deep into the tree's core – one of those odd things that happens during a tornado – something is placed completely out of context in the most startling locations.

It's okay. These are just flashbacks. You're safe now.

I walked back around to the front step. There was no door. No living room wall. They had all been blown out by the storm's force. I stepped over the threshold and once again drifted into the troubled nightmares of days long past. The living room was as grey and dark as my grandfather. A few jagged pieces of glass remained in the window frames throughout the house. From the front to the back, long sheets of brown, brittle cheese cloth hung loosely from the ceiling. They floated slowly in the air, like menacing sentinel spirits left behind to push me back into ancient dread.

I heard his piano playing. From the corner of my eye, the phantom piano appeared and there I sat. In his lap, locked on either side by his arms as he played and sang, "Have a Little Talk with Jesus." I felt him get hard through his trousers, through my dress. His smell, his shape, his voice – it was all so real. Too real.

I quickly moved away from the living room and deeper into the house. The music stopped, but the ceiling ghosts were everywhere. They waited for me. They were there, whispering about the resurrected the past that I was so vividly reliving by then. They had been there, tucked away until the storm. They knew. The whole house knew.

Like an abandoned child looking for a kind face, I wandered from room to room in the front portion of the house. Huge piles of broken glass, fallen ceiling debris, dirt, animal feces, a faded orange trick-or-treat pumpkin basket, a used condom, a plastic crucifix – the floor was littered with debris. The large windows throughout the house were made of two big panes that were raised and lowered by pulleys and cord. A few of them remained unbroken, but layers of weathered paint glued them shut, rendering them useless.

The next few rooms held little for me emotionally, except to serve as a point of reference. Snippets of meaningless information streamed through my conscious thoughts. *That's where the divan was. That's where we found a garden snake in the house. Here's where I played with my doll.* I reached the last room in the front of the house - I think it had been a small mud room on the far end that opened to the outside, looking toward the woods and ravine. Train whistles were often heard through those trees.

I turned to retrace my steps, then made my way to the kitchen where a toy gun lay on the counter top. This kitchen was my grandmother's kingdom. It was where her survival skills were honed. The place where her craft kept the beast pacified. In the purest sense of the word, she was an artist – a culinary artist. But in that kitchen, I couldn't smell her southern cooking. All I could smell was the mildew and dust of a broken house.

I stared into her sanctuary for quite awhile, and then the moldy, dead room came to life. On the wall appeared a wooden shadow box of a carved, three-dimensional kitchen that spoke of hearth and warmth and all that a family kitchen should be. As a child, I loved it. Now before me, on the instrument where the maestro played – her stove – was cornbread, fried chicken, mashed potatoes, and purple hull peas. And then, I heard it. *Clink. Clink. Clink.* He was tapping on his glass with a spoon – a signal for her to pour more sweet tea. Like a trained circus animal, she obeyed. She was his slave. I became full of rage at the degrading way he treated her. But as intense as that rage was, it paled in comparison to the disgust I felt for her passive compliance to his unchallenged demands. I shook my head to silence the clinking and the rage. The room returned to its lifeless state, the plastic gun on the counter and vigilant ceiling specters remained diligent over my awakened nightmares.

Then, in a matter of minutes, I was once more pulled back as a little girl by the monstrous time machine of flashbacks. I was back at the kitchen table, watching my grandmother cook breakfast. Something terrible had happened and I was upset. Very upset and very nervous. Grandpa sat next to me, drinking his first Coca-Cola of the day. I was fidgety. Squeamish. I quickly ate breakfast and then it happened. I vomited all over the kitchen table, making a huge and disgusting mess. A big mess. The vision jolted me to the point that I gulped for air and turned away from that child – turned away from me. The smells and sight of the vomit repulsed me. I desperately wanted to clean up that little girl, but I couldn't. She was on her own, just like she had been decades before.

I left her in her mess and went out to the back screened porch. I recalled stacks of wooden Coca-Cola cases next to stacks of cases holding empty bottles, waiting to be returned for their deposit. It was one of Grandpa's addictions. What space wasn't occupied by his Coke bottles was filled with large chest deep freezers that Grandmother kept filled with meats, vegetables, and fruit she had put up. I could hear the freezer motors' loud hums and felt the vibrations they sent through the porch floor boards. I looked out through the screen to the backyard, returning to the flashback of my terrified four year old brother being tormented by my grandfather. *"Stop it!"* I whispered, then spun around to go back into the house. Through the kitchen, I hurried into the long hallway.

High above me, the attic fan hung tenuously, exposed like a mutilated skeleton. Most of the attic had fallen down and shattered across the hallway, making it almost impossible to pass to the end of the hall. Boards lay with protruding rusty nails like booby traps waiting to be stepped on. It was treacherous. Each step caused more debris to shift. It was like walking on some far away glacier that threatened to give way over a deep ice crevice. If it collapsed, I might never be heard from again. I felt I was in tremendous danger.

The Locked Room

Even now, my memories are riddled with blank spaces. Dark holes that feel as if they contain monsters, yet maddeningly inaccessible. I have unanswered questions. There are circumstances that still make no sense to me. Glimpses of events dart across my consciousness, leaving only vapor trails that I do not understand.

I've grown to appreciate the insulating power of those blank spots. Throughout my journey, I've discovered that God pulls back the curtain when I'm ready. Ready to see. Ready to remember. Those memories and memory fragments have come at odd and unexpected times over the years. Some still remain unknown.

There was one such dark vacancy in my mind about an occurrence in a particular room of that house. Honestly, I hadn't remembered the existence of that room at all until I made my way to the end of the hallway. To my right was the bedroom where Grandpa regularly abused me. Directly in front of me – at the end of the hallway – was a small bathroom with an old metal shower stall, broken toilet, a sink hanging by one cold water fixture, and a caved in floor so that the earth underneath it was visible. Plants pushed through the broken places and a whole eco-system seemed to form there.

To my left was another bedroom. The sight of that closed door terrified me, but I couldn't remember why. I stood frozen between two rooms where my nightmares took place, staring at a bathroom where I cleaned myself up after he was finished with me. I reached out my left hand to turn the knob, which easily turned. When I tried to push it open I couldn't. In a house where the exterior walls were blown out, this room was bolted from the inside. A choking fear worked up through my throat. I shivered in terror, confused by this locked room with its unyielding secrets. The strips of ghostly ceiling cloths seemed agitated at this spot. They were longer and lower than at other points in the house, as if a large wild creature had shredded them with sharp claws. I panicked, wondering if that creature was lurking behind the bolted door, waiting for me.

Why was this door locked? Locked from the inside? It made no sense because the windows and walls were virtually gone. From the house's exterior, anyone could have walked into that room. There was no need to lock it. It was wide open to the outside world. A cloth ceiling spirit brushed against my head. My skin crawled as if thousands of spiders had just descended on me.

What happened in there? I struggled to remember, still holding the door knob. Faint images faded in, then faded away. There I was, sleeping on the floor, curled in a ball on some kind of blanket. My grandparents were in their beds. A dark figure was standing over me. I quickly jerked my hand away like the door knob had become white hot. No answers – only ominous shadows and images that still made no sense to me. These mysteries remained behind a door that was locked for no apparent reason. For the time being, that part of the past was still sealed off from my memories.

An Audience With God

The moment had come. I turned from the mystery room to face the open room of my abuse. The phantoms twisted and lurched like ghosts on a leash. I walked through the doorway, my breathing shallow and labored. To my right was a small closet. The door was partially opened. Was someone hiding inside waiting for me? There was nothing there except my paranoid fear. It was empty. Obliterated interior walls lay across the floor to my left, exposing another bathroom between here and the locked room. It was the bathroom of my grandparents' room. I could have walked through the wall studs and into that locked room, unhindered, but decided against it.

Farther to my left, on the back end of the room was an exterior door that opened to the back yard. Both the door and the screen door were wide open, wedged apart into a clear passage by swollen boards and rusted hinges. Like a mutating monster, blackberry vines from the yard had grown several feet into the room. They fanned out and wrapped around the pile of boards to block the exit.

Directly opposite of the bedroom door were two large windows, untouched by the tornado. The thick, bubbled glass remained intact. Through them, I could see the back porch that used to hold Grandpa's Coca-Cola and Grandmother's deep freezers. I moved around to the far corner of the room between the second window and the back wall. My steps were slow and deliberate. I turned to face the room, backed into the corner. From that perspective, the room suddenly closed in and imprisoned me. I pushed back hard against the wall for shelter, but it was too late. I drifted to the ceiling with the voyeur phantoms and together, we watched the little girl that once was me.

Twisted touch. Smells. Debilitating fear. Repulsive taste left in my mouth. Gagging. Textures. Fluids. Blistering pain. More than I will share took place in that dimly lit room beneath me. Like the child below, I could not bear to stay. In a flash, over forty years dissolved and I melted into my old familiar corner where I had often dissociated up to the ceiling. I spent many precious moments in that corner during Grandpa's visits. That's where I created my fantasy world. The little girl body remained below, enduring things no child should endure, but my spirit fled to that spot, always just in time to not go insane. The vessel that held my soul was broken, but the rest of me escaped like a refugee to the sanctuary of that ceiling corner just above the closet door.

From my vantage point, I watched the wretched conclusion to Grandpa's routine. Prayer. You see, he was a southern, Bible-thumping Christian evangelist – a music evangelist to be precise. People liked him. He was charismatic, smart, and revered by everyone. He spent his entire life holding revivals in small churches, saving the souls of sinners, winning the lost for Jesus. And what do pedophile evangelists do after they've violated a child? Well, I don't know what they all do, but Grandpa made me pray. He made me kneel down next to the bed where only moments before his unholy acts had shattered my little soul.

Jesus, help me to be a good girl. Jesus, please come into my heart so I won't go to hell. Jesus, please forgive me of my sins. Thank you for dying on the cross to save my soul.

So God is a part of this, too? That was a question that haunted me for years.

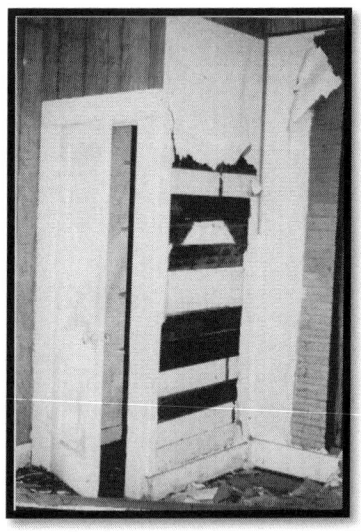

I drifted back down to my adult flesh, then made my way back to the bedroom door, hobbling slowly – just as I had done all those years ago. Just before I walked out, I froze. I hadn't seen it before. The tornado's destruction had weathered the room, stripping away the years of wall paper. Layer after layer were laid bare. Like a book of stamps on a humid day, they adhered to each other. I peeled them back until I got to the one I recognized. The one I stared at so often on my way up to the ceiling corner. I pealed it from the wall into a few small pieces. Most of them crumbled to dust in my hands, but two remained together and whole.

I turned to look once more at the frightened little girl, kneeling before her grandfather. I heard her pray, asking Jesus to come into her life and save her filthy soul. Hearing her ask Jesus to please let her go to heaven when she died, to please not send her to hell because she wasn't saved broke my heart. *One more night of an audience with God*, I thought.

The wounded child that I was grew into a teenager who decided I wanted nothing to do with *that* "god." The entanglement of my soul with Grandpa's god catapulted me into a toxic and perilous spiritual crisis so hate-filled, so enraged, that it impacted every aspect of my life.

Jesus had saturated my life as a child. Sunday School, church, prayer meetings, revivals, the Bible, and Gospel music comprised the foundation that our family was built upon. I was the master performer during Bible quizzes. I could find every book in the Bible quicker than any other child (and probably adult, for that matter!) during church Bible tournaments. God, Jesus, and Christianity – it was all inescapable for me. So was sexual abuse. As far as I could tell, they were all the same things: perversion and betrayal.

God was a cruel and twisted voyeur. God had betrayed me. That was my conclusion. So I set out to cauterize the spiritual wounds inflicted by Grandpa's god and seared them closed by walking away from Christianity.

Walking out of that room, there was a resurgence of old, familiar questions. *Where was God? Why did he allow this to happen?*

I remembered the Scripture where Jesus stated, "*I tell you, there is rejoicing in the presence of the angels of God over one sinner who repents*" (Luke 15:10).

Did Heaven rejoice when I repented with my grandfather? The past rage pulled hard at my spirit. As if trapped in a time warp vortex, I got into the hallway as fast as I could, leaving the bedroom and heading back toward the front door.

No Escape

It was September, 1962. We had been living in Arkadelphia for about six months and I was now in third grade. My father's deployment to Korea was half over, so he was able to take an R&R leave (rest and relaxation) for three weeks in Hawaii. I lay on Mother's bed, sifting through her tin of spare buttons and clasps as she packed for her trip to rendezvous there with him.

"Please don't go," I begged.

"I'll be home before you know it," she said.

"But why can't *we* go?"

"Because you're in school and Daddy and I need some time together, alone," she said. I began to cry. She continued to pack.

Before my Dad left for his yearlong hardship tour, my parents decided it would be nice for us to move close to family. Even though my maternal grandmother lived alone in Little Rock, Arkansas – about one hour from Arkadelphia – they decided we should move where my paternal grandparents lived. I think we had all hoped to have their love and support during this very difficult year of separation.

Mother's father died when she was very young, so a factor in this decision was our need to have a father-figure during Dad's absence. None of us realized what this decision would mean to the rest of my life. From the beginning, there was tension. Despite every effort on the part of my mother to have a functional relationship with Dad's parents, it was a toxic environment for all of us.

Like any other family, my brother and I went to our grandparents' house and spent many nights over there. Grandpa's sexual abuse had started long before this move, but once we settled there, it escalated just by the availability and access he had to me. And who would have thought anything about that? After all, isn't that what grandparents do? Don't they have sleepovers and help parents to raise children? His actions flew completely under everyone's radar.

Now, Mom was packed and I had moved my things to a neighbor's house rather than my grandparents' because she had already had so many vicious conflicts with my grandfather. In retrospect, everyone knew something wasn't right, but at the time, no one could fathom what that eerie feeling was really about. Mother separated me and my brother, and sent him to stay with other friends during her absence. He was almost four years old at the time. I was eight. Back then, there were no mobile communication devices, or the internet, or even direct calls that could have been made from the mainland to Hawaii. Once she left, we had no way of contacting her. No way of contacting each other.

As I recall, I liked the people I was staying with, but that didn't help me with the terror of being without my mother for three weeks. My father was gone, my brother was gone, and now my mother was gone. Our neighbors did the best they could to comfort me. One night, we watched the Miss American Pageant and I fantasized about being beautiful and talented as I watched Jacquelyn Mayer (Miss Ohio) walk down the runway to Bert Parks singing "There She Is, Miss America" on September 8, 1962. It was a Saturday night.

I went to bed, dreaming of tiaras and roses, but in the middle of the night, I awoke to horrible pain on my right side. I began vomiting profusely and doubling over in pain. Our neighbors rushed me to the Arkadelphia Hospital emergency room and by the next day, I had had an emergency appendectomy.

After the surgery, I was moved into a room that I shared with an elderly woman who was dying of cancer. She moaned and cried out constantly in pain. I, too, was in horrible pain, but was also just a young child – alone and sharing a hospital room with a dying woman. It was a nightmare, except it was real. The old lady died while I was in the room with her. I heard her last gasp and saw her tattered frame wheeled out of the room. Other than the nurses, I faced that experience alone.

I guess to keep me entertained, the nurses let me keep the scalpel used in my surgery, and every glass syringe – complete with the needle – after I received each shot. I had a Raggedy Ann doll that stayed with me through the traumatic hospital stay and she became my companion and witness to all that was happening to me. It was overwhelming for me, so I made it overwhelming for her. When I got a shot, I took the syringe and filled it with grape drink and gave her a shot, too. Before it was all said and done, we were both scared and scarred. She left the hospital covered in purple blotches, I left covered in red injection sites and a large incision in my abdomen.

Arkadelphia was a small town and everyone knew everyone, so when I was hospitalized, my grandparents were called. And why wouldn't they be? It made sense that they should be called, right? They were my grandparents. Soon, they began coming to the hospital. No one gave it a thought. I'm not sure what I understood about the arrangements at the time, but what I clearly understood was terror. All that time, my mother had no idea what had happened to me. She was in Hawaii having a much needed vacation with my dad.

It was nearing the time for me to be released and I knew what was about to happen. I was going home with my grandparents. I had to do something. I had to reach my mother and tell her to come home, but I didn't know how to do that. I didn't' know how to get in touch with her and no one would help me.

"I want my Mommy!" was met with, "She'll be home soon."

I found a dime and remembered seeing a pay phone down the hall. No one must know what I was planning, not even the nurses. I crawled out of bed and made my way down the corridor to the phone. I lifted the receiver and heard the coin clang as it sifted down through the pay phone's inner workings. I dialed "O" for the operator and when she answered, I began to sob.

"I want my Mommy! Please help me! She's in Hawaii and I need her to come get me!" I cried.

One of the nurses appeared, took the receiver and told the operator everything was alright, and then she escorted me back to bed. My coin was gone and so was my hope. I cannot describe that feeling of utter despair and abject dread. Soon it was time for my release and my grandparents arrived to take me to their house. No one thought a thing about it. A little girl whose mother was out of town belonged with her grandparents after major surgery, right?

Every cell in my body was filled with trepidation. We pulled up to their house and they carried me in. I was back in that house. Back in that bedroom. Back with the pedophile grandfather who led me in prayer. I had to get out, that much I was sure of, but how? When? I was completely disoriented as far as what day of the week it was or how long Mother had been gone or how long I'd been in the hospital. What I was completely clear about was my very real concern that he was going to come through that bedroom door any minute and begin the sexual routine.

I wasn't sure how much time I had left before that happened, so I made a decision. With the reasoning of a child and my body not yet fully recovered, there was only one option I could think of. I would wait until the house was dark, then escape, walk across town to my house, and wait in the carport for my mother to return. At last, my grandparents went to bed and he didn't come into my room that night. I knew it was now-or-never. I got dressed and quietly opened my bedroom door. As silently as I could, I started down the hallway. The enormous attic fan spun loudly, pulling air through the house. I hoped it would cover the sounds of my footsteps.

I found the front door and quietly turned the knob in the dark. And then, without warning, a hand appeared out of the darkness and pushed the door closed. It was my grandfather. To this day, I have no recollection of what happened next. What I do remember is being rushed to the doctor because my incision had pulled apart.

Decades later, I stood under that exposed attic fan, vividly remembering the threat, the terror, and the darkness that enveloped me that night. My hand dropped to my right side and I traced the thick and jagged scar on my belly left from that episode. Years later, when I was in my late thirty's, the scar became inflamed and something hard and metallic pushed its way through my skin. I have no idea if it was left by the surgeon or by what happened that night. I suppose some things are best left as foggy details.

In an almost déjà vu moment, I couldn't find my way out of that hallway. The next thing I remembered, I was in the car being driven back to Hot Springs.

The Lies Feel Like the Truth

For several days after my unexpected walkthrough, I felt disoriented and fearful. In a fog, I drifted back and forth between the past and the present. The eerie condition of the house – the debris, the ghostly ceiling cheesecloth, the exposed attic fan, the vines, the blown out walls, and the random items left behind affected me deeply. Darkly. My sleep was fitful. My mind, unfocused.

One night, shortly after I returned home, I got up to use the restroom. When I closed the bathroom door, before the light went on, I turned around and there he was. For a micro-second, my grandfather was there, staring at me with his hollow eyes, in my face with accusations. *You know you wanted it*, he hissed in the darkness and then, he vanished. I was reduced to that little girl all over again.

I did something to invite the abuse. Why else would he have done such things? I was a filthy, twisted girl. I made it all up – it couldn't be true. Everyone loved him, loved my grandmother. I was evil to even think such things about him.

It took me hours to calm down from the apparition.

I had been on this journey beyond abuse long enough to know I need to get help outside of my own thoughts. I needed to make myself accountable to people I trusted. My husband, Tim, had already been through so much turmoil and misdirected rage from me. I could see the dread on his face as I'm sure he knew we were in for some rough days ahead. There was also something else I saw in his face – compassion and empathy. There were long, difficult moments in the middle of the night. We had many conversations about my walk-through, and also had many moments of absolute silence as we both got lost in our thoughts, waiting for what would come next. I took great comfort in his stability and belief in me.

For days, I heard the ceiling ghosts of brown floating cheesecloth put me on trial, as if I stood naked before my accusers. *Look at you! What have you done? Everyone knows because it shows. Everyone can tell. You're trashed – just like the house. There's nothing left. You're broken down and overgrown with so much debris, there's no hope for you. No one else has done what you've done. You're alone and you're destroyed.*

I called two close friends, Paula and Cathy, who had been an important part of my own journey and in the developing work of Committed to Freedom. Both were abuse survivors. Both knew the lies that screamed in my head. Both refused to ignore the turmoil I was in. They came alongside me – encouraging, accompanying, and caring.

I immersed myself in passages of Scripture that brought comfort and strength to me.

You, dear children, are from God and have overcome them, because the one who is in you is greater than the one who is in the world (1 John 4:4).

I have told you these things, so that in me you may have peace. In this world you will have trouble. But take heart! I have overcome the world (John 16:33).

I can do all this through him who gives me strength (Philippians 4:1).

I used my voice to seek wisdom and strength in prayer, to express my needs to those I relied on, and to remind myself of truth – no matter how loud the lies were screaming at me in my head. I surrounded myself with symbols, music, film, quotes, items that brought comfort, and art pieces that spoke to me. Like a warrior princess wielding a magic sword, I used these as tangible talismans of truth in order to combat the lies. I used everything we teach at Committed to Freedom to bring truth back into focus, and I held on for dear life to these tools and these people during that process.

There was one particular phrase from the New Testament that kept me grounded. It was an invitation from Jesus, found in Matthew 11:28, where he said, *"Come to me, all you who are weary and burdened, and I will give you rest."* Like a mantra, I said it again and again, and I remembered another time many years before when that invitation literally saved my life.

Awakened by the Artist

I was seventeen, living in Williamsburg, Virginia – an ancient place that readily fed my hunger for mystical experiences. It is a place where dead things are highly revered, where a way of life rests in the histories of human passing. I obsessed over the antiquities and delved into a dark spirituality there. I found certain ancient witchcraft practices be very empowering. It felt deeply spiritual and profoundly metaphysical in ways that helped me to put as much distance as possible between my soul and the perverted Christianity of my grandparents.

I believed I had found a way to manipulate people and events, and that ability gave me exactly what I wanted in order to gather power. It was a very heady concept for a girl who had known such powerlessness and it was far removed from a cruel, abusive voyeur god. I could feel my strength growing with my practice. I felt very connected to my feminine power. I felt dangerous and I adored that feeling.

The certainty that I was in control diverted my attention away from how broken I was. In reality, I was slipping farther and farther out of control as the lies from the abuse punctured my spirit. It didn't matter how much power I had, how much I thought I could manipulate people or circumstances, at the end of the day, I still felt like a disgusting piece of garbage. Whatever my emerging mystical powers were, they were built upon a foundation of abuse, exploitation, terror, and lies from my past.

There was a growing cacophony of self-loathing in my head. What had been whispers as a child snowballed into violent inner tirades that shredded me. I couldn't shut them up, no matter how many incantations I said or rituals I practiced. I had slipped off the ledge of reason and plummeted into a dark abyss with no bottom. I was hopeless. In my mind I had nothing left to give, nothing left to be taken. I was done, and not only was I done, but I had no place to go with that despair. You see, when your back is against the wall and God is your enemy, you're in a very hopeless place – and I was.

A dark presence wrapped itself around me and choked me with boa constrictor fear that slowly coiled around my soul and squeezed the life out of me. I was a filthy, defiled, evil piece of trash, betrayed by God and now betrayed by the promises of magical spirituality that I had been pursuing. Nothing helped. I was in so much pain that I had to do something. My thinking was muddy and irrational. I was so confused that suicide seemed to be the only solution to make the noise shut up.

In Colonial Williamsburg, there are many graveyards. I especially loved the one at Bruton Parish church. Large table tombs lay above ground, embellished with images and epitaphs to venerate the dead. There was one in particular that I loved – the table tomb of Robert Rae who died in 1753. That's where I decided I would end my life – laying on his table tomb.

My parents had no idea about the abuse or about how unstable I had become. No one did. The only one who could hear the voices was me and the chaos had become unbearable. Sleeping pills and razor blades would finally relieve my torment and silence the voices. I had to die and face the perverted voyeur deity, myself. At the time, that seemed reasonable.

It was a cold January night when I walked through my house for the last time. I paused to take it all in one more time before I disappeared into the night, forever. The television was tuned in to a national news program which played to an empty living room. It was 1971 and religious communes were springing up all over the country. Communes like *Jesus People USA* had rejected conventional church to embrace Jesus as a pacifist revolutionary and a social radical. I found their approach appealing, but not to the point that I had taken more than a passing notice of their message.

That night, the journalist was covering another religious commune called the *Children of God**. They were interviewing their leader, Moses David (*David Berg*), about his group and why they had chosen to drop out of society and live communally. He was incredibly charismatic – so much so that he caught my attention and I paused to listen to what he had to say. The long haired, bushy bearded face of a bright eyed young man with beads and a guitar filled the screen. He spoke of Jesus in ways that were new to me. He spoke of God's love and friendship. He referred to Jesus as a revolutionary, one he followed, and someone who had made a difference in his life. He spoke of counter-cultural passion and love and peace – he spoke to me and it felt earnest and authentic.

To this day, I don't fully understand what happened as I listened to that interview, but a paradigm shift took place in my soul as a raging war erupted between two versions of Jesus: Jesus the perverted voyeur and Jesus the radical revolutionary of love and peace. I ran outside into the cold Virginia night and began screaming at God. I was in spiritual agony and it was tearing me apart. I was certain insanity would overtake me at any moment.

Hot tears drained from my eyes. I was exhausted and I collapsed to the ground, sobbing. My sobs slowed to crying. My crying slowed to a dry whimper. And then I was still. That's when I noticed it – the spectacular night sky. It was peppered with brilliant stars and a sentinel moon. That beauty gave birth to an epiphany: the artist capable of creating such a night sky could not, in any way, be the perverted creature my grandfather had introduced me to.

I once heard Robert Kennedy, Jr. being interviewed about God. He said, *"If you want to know about Michelangelo, you can read about him in a book, but if you really want to KNOW him, go lie on the floor of the Sistine Chapel – then you'll know Michelangelo. The same can be said of God. If you want to know God, you can read that information in a book, but if you really want to KNOW God, go immerse yourself in nature and creation – then you'll know God."*

That night, I was surrounded by a spectacular celestial show that filled me with a deep sense of awe and sent peace radiating down deep into my soul. The interview altered how I thought about Jesus and that night sky altered me. Puffs of warm air escaped from my lungs to fade in wisps of white vapor. I closed my eyes and heard a whisper come out of my mouth, "Jesus, help me." Simple. Quiet. Honest.

As if suddenly immersed in a deep, warm tub of water, my whole body radiated with tranquility. Every ounce of rage and tension melted, replaced by the most serene peace I had ever known.

"*I am the Message,*" my spirit heard, "*I am different than the messengers.*"

I understood. It finally made sense to me. I stepped back from all the lies, the confusion, the shame and guilt, and I saw it clearly. Jesus was different from the monster who claimed to work for him. The *Message* was different than the perverted messengers. One had nothing to do with the other. I could separate the two. I saw the one who sinned against me for who he was – a hijacker of faith, body, and soul – and I saw Jesus for who he was – a peaceful revolutionary who could show me the way forward. They were two entirely different entities.

To this day, I struggle with religious labels that attempt to contain spiritual shifts in one's soul, but I suppose what happened to me could be called *salvation*. It could be understood as my being *born again* – because I was given another chance. Spiritually, I became a follower of Jesus and I made the choice to walk away from the darkness and into light. That night, I didn't die. I changed. I started to live.

*Years later, the Children of God disbanded and were accused of being a mind-control cult where sexual exploitation and abuse were rampant, but at the time – all I heard were Moses David's words of peace, love, and Jesus the revolutionary – and it changed my life.

Staring Down the Demons

...and I lived happily ever after. The End.

Oh, it would be nice to tell you that from that night on, my life was great and everything from my past had been resolved, but the truth is that I carried a lot of heavy baggage because of the abuse and my life circumstances, and I made sure those bags stayed closed and locked. My spiritual enlightenment had not undone the damage. It would take me years to understand that. I dragged every bit of that damage into my new life as a Christ-follower.

I also did what many good Christians do with troubling issues that aren't easily fixed. I stuffed them down deep where no one would see. Where no one would know. I never opened those twisted broken places to the healing peace of Christ's love, never ventured into the darkness with the spiritual light that values truth. I bought into the mentality that if I wasn't immediately whole, then I didn't have enough faith – and that was something I couldn't bear to even think was possible. I had found hope and life and I didn't want to do anything to rock that illusionary boat. I remained full of neatly tucked away shame and guilt, and over the years, it began to fester.

About six months after that life changing night, we moved to the Philippines where I would graduate from high school. As soon as we arrived in country, I heard about a youth prayer and Bible study group, and decided to join. The first time I went, I met a gorgeous young man named Tim who was also about to begin his senior year of high school. Honestly, I think it was love at first sight for me. It took Tim a few more months to realize the chemistry between us, but on February 12, 1972, he kissed me for the first time and that was it. We've been together ever since.

When we came back to the United States to go to college, we eloped before the end of our freshman year. By then we were nineteen years old and knew that the world was ours for the taking. Ours was going to be a fairy tale life - the same kind of *happily ever after ending* that I thought was the way that following Christ was supposed to pay off. But intimacy and the pressure of day-to-day living had quite the opposite result. The festering bitterness and unresolved issues I lugged into our relationship exploded all over the love of my life and it was ugly.

Please understand that we were very young and completely unprepared for the volatile complications that my history with abuse had on how we functioned as a couple. I can tell you now that I needed someone to pay for what had been done to me. I didn't know it at the time, but that's exactly what I was doing. Somebody had to pay and it was Tim who received that unjust sentence. I was raging against the only person that was close enough for me to get away with it – my husband.

I was also doing something else. Again, please keep in mind that I can share the reasons for my actions at this point in my journey, but at the time, I had no idea what motivated me to behave in such a brutal way. The other thing I was doing was confirming my value. You see, despite the shift in my spiritual paradigm, at my core I still believed I was a piece of trash, worthy of being treated with no dignity or respect. After all, based on the actions of my grandparents, I couldn't have been worth very much, right? And so I set out to confirm my worth by pushing my husband to limits that would have caused a lesser person to break. I bullied and raged and pushed, pushed, pushed to evoke his retaliation – to get him to push back hard and hurt me. If he did, then he would have confirmed my value. He would have also confirmed my cynical expectation that everyone is ultimately out to betray and wound me.

The damage from my abuse was on a deadly trajectory, but at the time, neither of us understood what was happening. We limped along, thrashing like blind puppies starved for affection and food. I became a self-righteous raging maniac. I was relentless in my obsession with control and as a result, I systematically chipped away at our relationship and this wondrous man.

My heart's desire was to follow Christ and live by his teachings of peace, joy, love, and respect. Instead I became like the people who crucified Jesus – I lived my spiritual life in such a way that I trampled everyone around me. I was angry, bitter, smug, self-righteous, rigid, and contemptuous. Despite it all, Tim continued to love me, no matter what. I remember him calmly excusing himself when I went on rampages and telling me to let him know when I was finished so we could talk about whatever the issue was. I remember him saying to me, "I love you, but I won't be your victim." He never retaliated and he never confirmed my beliefs about myself.

From the outside, we were a cute young couple who devoutly served Christ. But on the inside, an angry cloud obstructed our view of each other and even of God. And then the day came that forced me to look in the mirror. We were at a church function. Three years of marriage had passed. We were all of twenty-one years old. For some reason, the topic of sexual abuse came up in a conversation. I heard myself blurt out in a deliberately casual way, "I was sexually abused."

The people around us were astonished. I felt proud of myself that I was so together that they had no idea. I expected a flurry of reactions that validated my fine Christian character, but I guess they were unsure what to say after such a disclosure. Instead, one person in the group asked a question that was almost as pivotal as that starry night a few years earlier in Williamsburg. She asked, "And it hasn't affected you in any way?"

I blew it off and said, "No! It hasn't! I'm a Christian, old things have passed away, all things have become new, remember?"

Then, I turned toward my husband for validation to my claim. My look was his cue to jump in and tell everyone what a perfect Christian I was. He didn't. He was silent with a look of shock on his face. His silence enraged me and as I glared at him, I saw something I was unprepared to see. I saw hurt, beat-down hurt in the eyes of my beautiful young husband. I had torn him down, degraded and berated him for three years. Looming back at me from those crystal blue eyes was pain, and in them I saw a reflection of the monster I was becoming.

And the Mask Came Off

The essence of abuse is the belief, followed by the actions, of someone who thinks they have the right to mishandle another being. I had spent most of my childhood and adolescence determined to never be anything like my grandfather. When I became a follower of Jesus, I wanted to be a reflection of him and his teachings. But the day I saw pain in my husband's eyes as a result of my behavior, I recognized that the image stamped in my heart was not that of Jesus. It was that of my abuser. I resembled him more than I reflected Christ.

Songs on the radio told us that all we needed was love, but it turned out, we needed a bit more than that.

I didn't understand. I couldn't solve the puzzle. I was exposed and once again unraveling, despite my faith and my lifestyle changes. How could this be? Had God failed me again? The short answer to that last questions is *no*. The long answer involves understanding the beauty and value of having to confront myself, no matter how ugly, painful, or unfair that process may have been.

This time, I not only had a profound moment of enlightenment, but I had matured enough to recognize that my good intentions were not enough. I had to roll up my sleeves and go to work, recognizing that the life I was fighting for was mine.

I made some decisions that formed the framework for what was ahead. First, I was going to pursue truth. I didn't need to shrink back. I needed to be honest about everything. There was so much more that had happened to me that I hadn't come to terms with yet. There was also a great deal of damage I had done to myself as I acted out in my youth. One of the most terrifying prayers I ever prayed was, "God, I give you permission to hold up a mirror and let me truly see."

There was and is so much I don't understand about God or faith, but one thing I hold on to with great conviction is that the path of truth I chose was my destined passage to health and balanced well-being. Obviously the actions (and inactions) of my grandparents played a substantial role in who I had become. What *they* did was *their* responsibility and *their* guilt, not mine. But I also knew full well that I had to take responsibility for my own choices and stop blaming my tyrannical way of living on my abuse. Gradually, with this resolve to live authentically, the death grip of lies and shame began to loosen.

And so my journey began, but where to begin? How do I proceed? Where was I going and when would I know I had arrived? I didn't know who to turn to for help because I honestly didn't know what I needed. The first people I turned to were clergy and spiritual leaders. In many ways, I think they were completely unprepared for the depths of my damage or the hard questions I was asking.

Rejecting the Magic Wand

Unfortunately, I have learned over the years that sometimes when people – good people – don't know what to say or are extremely uncomfortable with my truth, they can cause a lot of unintentional harm. I started hearing instructions like, "Give it to God, Sallie."

Okay, I'd love to do that, but what exactly does that mean? I thought I had, but now you're telling me I haven't. I felt like that kid who is on the outside with her nose pressed against the window pane, looking inside at others who evidently know a secret I don't know.

So that advice didn't go over too well. What else have you got?

"Well, you need to have more faith and pray harder!"

Why? Because God's stupid? Because I haven't come up with the right incantation or formula or ritual to convince God that I need help? That's rubbish. I don't need to manipulate God to find peace and wholeness. I need to feel connected and spiritually plugged in.

One of my favorite authors, Anne Lamott, writes that there are only two kinds of prayers you need to know: *Help Me, Help Me, Help Me* and *Thank You, Thank You, Thank You.* The instructions I was being given reeked of a belief that God wasn't capable of understanding my anguish or needs. I rejected that and spent a lot of time with the very precise and concise prayer of *Help Me, Help Me, Help Me*, certain that that was enough for God to understand what I meant.

So that advice didn't go over too well, either. Anything else you'd like to share?

"It's obvious, Sallie. You need to forgive and forget."

Okay, I'll be honest. That one just about sent me lunging over the sacred desk.

Look, I know you mean well, and it's obvious that forgiveness is an important part of this journey I'm on, but to pretend I have amnesia and call it forgiveness is a cheap substitute for the gut wrenching reality that I was violated, injured, and have scars. That's not faith, that's denial and I've already tried that. It doesn't work for long. It squishes sideways and can do a lot of harm. In fact, I think that the sign of a mature Christian is one who can look at atrocity, full faced, and embrace the horror and damage and then point to it and say, *THAT* happened and I choose to forgive *THAT*.

Whew. This wasn't going to be easy. I needed knowledgeable guides, and just because there was a "Reverend" sign on the door, didn't necessarily mean they had the directions I needed. So the quest continued. I was determined to figure out how to move beyond what had happened to me. I was determined to reclaim my life and find my personal empowerment, to lay claim to my soul and refuse to settle for simplistic mumbo-jumbo when I needed real help and naked honesty.

I needed voices other than my own, so I began to read everything I could get my hands on about sexual abuse and recovery. I told my husband everything – *everything* – things that will never make it into a book or be told in public. When I told him, I was quite literally stunned that I didn't fall over dead. I began to scour Scriptures to see if they contained clues as to how I could find healing and balance. I began waiting in meditation and prayer, cultivating a spirit that was quiet and focused. And I began talking to my family about what had happened – which was more difficult than I could have ever imagined.

I went back to school and educated myself in psychology, theology, and counseling. Day by day, I opened my life up to knowledge, truth, and new perspectives. Pin pricks of light became beams of hope in my darkness and the mystery of *me* began to unravel. I was changing. My husband knew it, my children benefited from it, and I felt it. Shame was losing. Freedom was within my reach.

I finally took a giant vulnerable leap into the unknown when I decided to see a counselor. As much hard work as I had done on my own, I still needed a skilled guide to help me find my way through the maze of abuse and the issues I struggled with. Another important lesson came through that experience –not every therapist is right for me, and just because someone is a *Christian* therapist doesn't necessarily mean that he or she is a good therapist.

One Christian therapist I went to gave me an assignment that enraged me. She instructed me to write a letter to *little Sallie* and tell her that she was safe and that Jesus was with her. In our session, I was compliant, but when I left that office and started to think about the task I'd been given, I was enraged. I came back the next session and reported on my assignment: *Little Sallie* and I are confused. How is it that Jesus can be with *little Sallie* now that it's over, and hadn't been there for her during the abuse?

Little Sallie and I never went back. Just like everything else, it took time to find a therapist that was a good fit for me. I had to learn not to be intimidated by the license on the wall and the books in the library. I discovered I needed to challenge techniques and direction that made no sense to me. In many ways, that became an exercise in finding my voice and my personal empowerment.

The therapists I found gently and skillfully turned on a flashlight and directed me through some very dark passages. We opened closets where I had been keeping my well-fed monsters. We caged them, starved them, and I learned to turn a deaf ear to their savage hungers.

The great stabilizer through all of this was my husband. He could have given up on me, and probably should have. Now please understand that Tim arrived in our relationship with his own issues and baggage, so this wasn't about the perfect man fixing the very broken damsel in distress. He didn't deserve to be the recipient of wrath that should have been reserved for my abuser, but he often was.

One of the greatest gifts that Tim gave to me was his refusal to play my manipulative, bullying games. I pushed, and pushed hard. He didn't retaliate. I wanted to provoke him and engage in conflicts. He never stooped to my level. With integrity and courage, he loved me, was faithful to me, but would not indulge my tantrums. At the time, his refusal to engage infuriated me, but as I reflect back from the other side of the nightmare, it was a profound, wise, and compassionate response to my thrashing in pain.

It didn't happen overnight. It didn't even happen over weeks or even months. But as I looked back over decades of making choices, of choosing to reflect the love of Christ rather than the monster of my abuser, I began to see a different image in me. I have made many, many mistakes. I have slipped backwards to unhealthy coping behavior and bitterness more times than I'd like to admit. But with each success, I felt tiny new spiritual muscles toning. Like a body builder, the strength I have today came from those first few painful years when every breath and choice took a monumental effort. There were days when I was so tired of the battle that I wanted to give up. That's when the resources of education, meditation and prayer, counseling, support, and truth shored me up and gave me the strength to fight for what was mine.

All of this had been the backdrop to my walking into that demolished house in Arkadelphia. What I thought was going to be a simple filming of a promotional piece in front of this small, insignificant house, became yet another turning point and a moment of choice.

Were the accusing voices going to take me down again? Were the memories going to overtake me? Was the monster going to win?

These were legitimate questions in the weeks that followed that eventful day and I felt darkness trying to crowd back in and rob me blind.

"So what are you going to do?" asked my friend, Paula.

That question came after I shared that I had seen the apparition of my grandfather in the bathroom and felt I had been catapulted back into that vivid place of being a broken child. I wrestled with all of it. I prayed. I pulled out all the tools I had been teaching to others for years and I put them to work. It was exhausting, but I was absolutely certain of this one thing: I wasn't losing again.

"I'm going back to the house and I'm going to stare down my demons," I concluded.

Someone Else's Rubble

The first time I had gone to the house was when I randomly located it because I had time to kill one Saturday morning. The second time was when I returned and unexpectedly found it obliterated. A few weeks after that, I went to the house for the third time, accompanied by my husband, my daughter Anne, and a camera man.

On our way there, I spoke about how the last visit had impacted me and the oddness of that mystery room with the locked door. The drive was pretty quiet – reflective and solemn. Anne – an artist and photographer – had grown up while *Committed to Freedom* was forming. She would document the house through still photos. My husband came to offer support and perhaps for answers, too. The cameraman, a friend who was well acquainted with my journey and the importance of this moment, would shoot the video.

We drove past the cemetery until the street reached the dead end and parked in front of the house. My daughter loaded her camera with film. Tim squeezed my hand and we got out. The day was cloudy and mild.

By the broken magnolia tree, we paused to stare into the house whose walls had been blasted off. Tim slowly moved in closer and then stepped into the house. I could almost hear his thoughts as he, too, stood in the place that had impacted his life in profound and intimate ways. No one will ever know the price Tim paid for the actions of my grandfather. No one but Tim and God. I could only imagine. It wasn't fair. The far reaching injustice when a predator strikes cannot be overstated. Tim fought an invisible war with an invisible nemesis that might be compared to shadow boxing.

Injustice is one of those things you have to take a deep breath over and accept. If you don't, you'll be paralyzed by the actions of others. I resolved that issue long ago. Life isn't fair. This battle hadn't been fair either. Not for me. Not for my husband. Not for my family. The narrative of Jesus' experiences also informed me of injustice and I relied heavily upon that narrative to teach me how to move beyond my rage and bitterness.

For all of us, stepping across that threshold was akin to explorers landing on a distant planet. Each member of our party slowly moved through the house, room by room, trying to take in every detail, imagining the unimaginable. I was more or less prepared for my third visit. I wasn't overshadowed by shock and flashbacks like the last time, but I could see that it impacted everyone else that way now.

I entered the house empowered with the same resolve that I had when I began working on my healing journey. I had drawn a line in the sand. I had no doubt that I was no longer a victim and that my life was not reflected in that torn apart structure. This was knowledge that I found to be extremely energizing. The lies were exposed as lies. The truth was revealed and embraced as truth.

We shot video and still photographs. I escorted the people I love through each room, sharing stories about what happened in each one. *Here's where this happened. Here's where that happened. This is where I hid. This is where I cleaned up. This is where I got caught. This is where I played. This is where I disappeared.*

Like visitors at Auschwitz, they were haunted by what their imaginations filled in with each anecdote I told. I shared only scattered details, careful to give them time to process their own thoughts and feelings. I was very concerned for my husband and daughter as I watched their eyes, expression, and body language. Up until that day, my stories hovered in abstract clouds. Being in that place, walking through that place – now it was concrete and tangible. Together, we journeyed through the house, what I had experienced, and down the familiar path of mutual support and comfort.

I thought I had seen all there was to see in the house, but there was another surprise waiting for me. The door of that locked mystery room had been kicked in. Since my last visit, someone had broken down the door and left it splintered and shattered. Bizarrely, one large piece of that door had been neatly leaned against the far wall near all the blown out windows and skeletal wall studs. So I walked into the room through the shattered door frame to a room that held a terrifying experience I couldn't fully recall.

It was interesting that when I entered the room, I felt completely safe with no trepidation. The room was filled with light. The collapsed walls left large open spaces to the outside. Whether or not those memories will ever return to me in tact I cannot say, but even those shadows no longer owned me.

After spending hours in the house, we felt we had accomplished what we came there to do: document the journey beyond abuse. I walked out of the house and back into the yard. It was a powerful sensation to do that with my husband and daughter by my side.

Like squirming, dying vermin giving it one more try, I heard a stubborn lie drift through the house and out to me. *You still look like the house.* I smiled to myself and laughed under my breath. I whispered loud enough for hell to tremble and heaven to celebrate, "You're talking about someone else's rubble, not mine."

We packed our equipment, got in the car, and drove home. That night, I slept like a baby.

About a year later, my parents had flown in for a brief visit. They had slowly come to terms with what my grandfather had done not only to me, but others. Both of my grandparents were dead by then. Mom and Dad asked me to drive them to the house – they wanted to see it for themselves. I think they needed closure too, so I found myself driving to visit the house for the fourth time, anticipating that this would be a very difficult experience for my parents.

Again, we drove down the road, past the cemetery to where the road dead ends, but yet another surprise awaited us. The house was gone. The shell had been leveled – bulldozed into a mound of broken boards. The land was being cleared and most likely, something new would go up one of these days. It seemed to be the final gift from this poetic parallel.

All that remained was a pile of rubble. Someone else's rubble.

*Therefore, since we have so great a cloud of witnesses surrounding us, let us also lay aside every encumbrance, and the sin which so easily entangles us, and let us run with endurance the race that is set before us, fixing our eyes on Jesus the author and perfector of faith, who for the joy set before him endured the cross, **despising the shame**, and has sat down at the right hand of the throne of God. For consider him who has endured such hostility by sinners against himself, so that you may not grow weary and lose heart.*

– Hebrews 12:1-3 (New Testament Bible)

About Sallie Culbreth

Sallie Culbreth is the founder of Committed to Freedom – a non-profit organization that facilitates holistic empowerment and spiritual tools to help people move beyond abuse, exploitation, and sexual trauma, and provides adjunct services to helping professionals, agencies, and faith communities working with those who want to include spiritual concerns in their abuse recovery process. Her work and writings come from her personal experience of childhood sexual abuse and recovery. She holds a bachelor's degree in pastoral ministries and a master's degree in mental health counseling. She is a member of the American Psychological Association, American Association of Christian Counselors, and has received training in Critical Incidence Stress Management. She has authored several books and self-help workbooks and writes a weekly blog, Roadside Assistance.

She lives with her husband, Tim, in Hot Springs, Arkansas. They have two adult children and one grandchild.

Made in the USA
San Bernardino, CA
04 April 2014